The Medieval World

Children and Games
in the Middle Ages

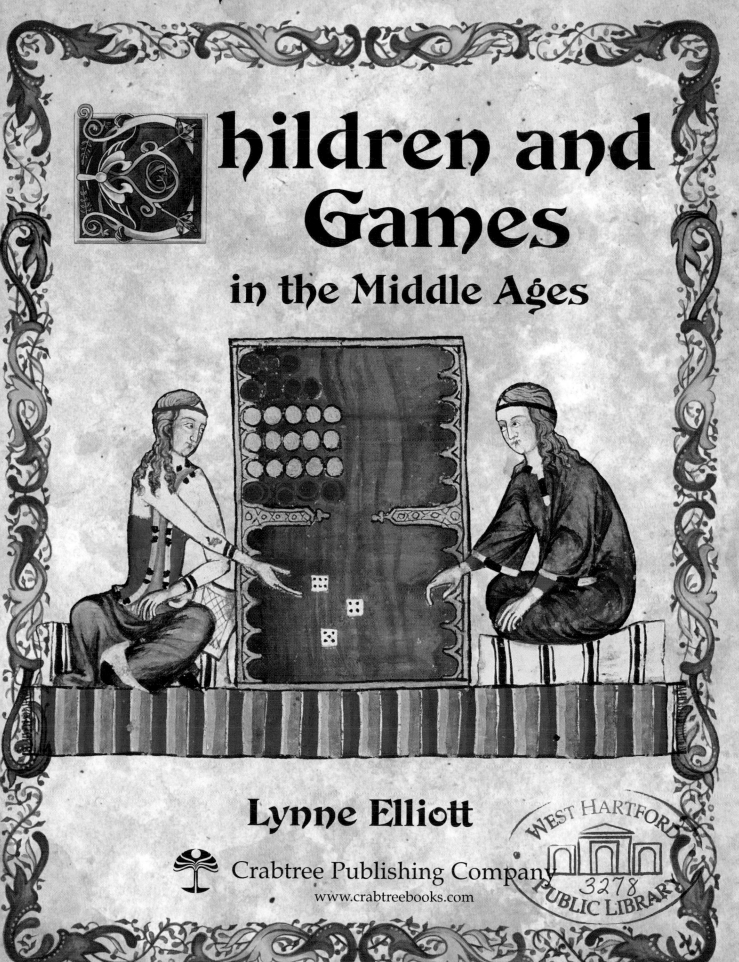

Lynne Elliott

Crabtree Publishing Company
www.crabtreebooks.com

Crabtree Publishing Company

www.crabtreebooks.com

Coordinating editor: Ellen Rodger

Project editor: Carrie Gleason

Designer and production coordinator: Rosie Gowsell

Scanning technician: Arlene Arch-Wilson

Art director: Rob MacGregor

Project development, editing, photo editing, and layout:
First Folio Resource Group, Inc.: Tom Dart, Jaimie Nathan,
Debbie Smith, Anikó Szocs

Photo research: Maria DeCambra

Prepress and printing: Worzalla Publishing Company

Consultant: Isabelle Cochelin, University of Toronto

Photographs: Alinari/Art Resource, NY: p. 14 (top right); Archivo
Iconografico, S.A./Corbis/magmaphoto.com: p. 19, p. 26
(bottom); Art Archive/Biblioteca d'Ajuda Lisbon/Dagli Orti: p. 13
(left); Art Archive/Biblioteca Estense Modena/Dagli Orti: p. 16,
p. 26 (top); Art Archive/Bodleian Library Oxford/Bodley 264
folio 95r: p. 9 (bottom); Art Archive/Bodleian Library Oxford/
Bodley 264 folio 112r: p. 8 (bottom right); Art Archive/Bodleian
Library Oxford/Douce 93 folio 28r: p. 31 (bottom); Art Archive/
Bodleian Library Oxford/Douce 195 folio 4: p. 27 (right); Art
Archive/Bodleian Library Oxford/Douce 276 folio 124v: p. 8 (top
center); Art Archive/British Library: p. 15 (top right); Art
Archive/Musée Condé Chantilly/Dagli Orti: p. 28; Art Archive/
Private Collection/Dagli Orti: p. 4; Art Archive/Real Biblioteca de
lo Escorial/Dagli Orti: title page, p. 12 (top); Art Archive/Real
Monasterio del Escorial Spain/Dagli Orti: p. 9 (top); Art Archive/
Saint Sebastian Chapel Lanslevillard Savoy/Dagli Orti: p. 7
(bottom left); Art Archive/San Agostino San Gimignano/Dagli
Orti: p. 24 (right); Art Archive/University Library Heidelberg/
Dagli Orti: p. 17 (top left); Art Archive/University Library
Prague/Dagli Orti: p. 13 (right); Art Archive/Victoria and Albert
Museum London/Graham Brandon: p. 20; Asian Art &
Archaeology, Inc./Corbis/magmaphoto.com: p. 17 (bottom right);
Bibliothèque Mazarine, Paris, France/Archives Charmet/
Bridgeman Art Library: p. 23 (bottom); British Library/Add.
38126 f. 7: p. 22; British Library/Topham-HIP/The Image Works:
p. 21 (bottom right); Centre Historique des Archives Nationales,
Paris, France/Lauros/Giraudon/Bridgeman Art Library: p. 15
(bottom left); École Nationale Vétérinaire, Maisons-Alfort,
France/Archives Charmet/Bridgeman Art Library: p. 7 (top
right); Giraudon/Art Resource, NY: p. 14 (bottom left), p. 18 (top);
Glasgow University Library, Scotland/Bridgeman Art Library:
p. 21 (top left); Erich Lessing/Art Resource, NY: p. 6 (top right),
p. 8 (left), p. 23 (top), p. 30, p. 31 (top); Mary Evans Picture
Library: p. 24 (left), p. 25, p. 27 (left); Musée Condé, Chantilly,
France/Giraudon/Bridgeman Art Library: p. 29; Réunion des
Musées Nationaux/Art Resource, NY: p. 12 (bottom), p. 18
(bottom); Scala/Art Resource, NY: cover

Illustrations: Barbara Bedell: p. 27; Jeff Crosby: pp. 10–11;
Katherine Kantor: flags, title page (border), copyright page
(bottom), p. 6 (bottom); Margaret Amy Reiach: borders, gold
boxes, title page (illuminated letter), copyright page (top),
contents page (all), pp. 4-5 (timeline), p. 5 (all), p. 32 (all)

Cover: On weekends and holidays, children in the Middle Ages
accompanied their parents to picnics, feasts, and other special
celebrations.

Title page: Children in the Middle Ages played board games such
as backgammon. The goal of backgammon is to be the first player
to remove all one's checkers from the backgammon board.

Crabtree Publishing Company

www.crabtreebooks.com   1-800-387-7650

Cataloging-in-Publication Data
Elliott, Lynne.
  Children and games in the Middle Ages / Lynne Elliott.
    p. cm. -- (The medieval world)
Includes bibliographical references (p. 32) and index.
  ISBN 0-7787-1349-0 (RLB) -- ISBN 0-7787-1381-4 (pbk)
  1. Amusements--History--To 1500--Juvenile literature. 2.
Games--History--To 1500--Juvenile literature. 3. Children-
-Social life and customs--Juvenile literature. I. Title. II.
Medieval world (Crabtree Publishing Company)
  GV41.E55 2004
  796.093--dc22

                                         2004000730
                                            LC

J
940.1
ELLIOTT
J
3/08

**Published in
the United States**
PMB 16A
350 Fifth Ave.,
Suite 3308
New York, NY
10118

**Published
in Canada**
616 Welland Ave.,
St. Catharines,
Ontario, Canada
L2M 5V6

**Published in the
United Kingdom**
73 Lime Walk,
Headington,
Oxford
0X3 7AD
United Kingdom

**Published
in Australia**
386 Mt. Alexander Rd.,
Ascot Vale (Melbourne)
V1C 3032

Table of Contents

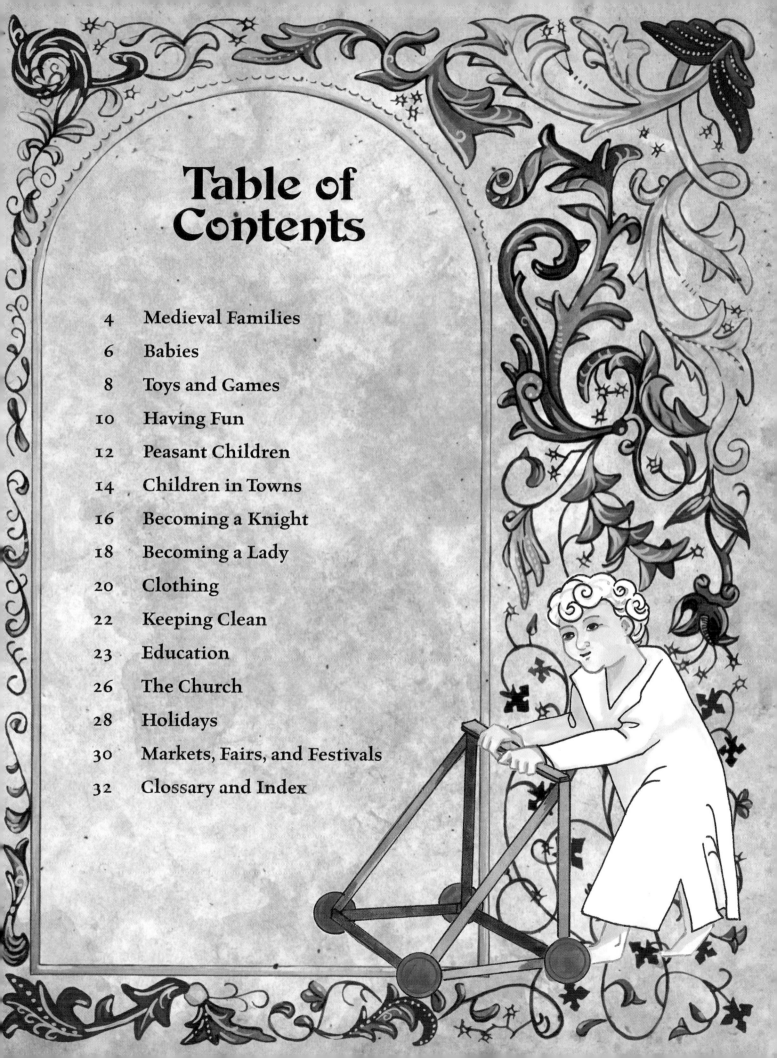

Medieval Families

The Middle Ages lasted from 500 A.D. to 1500 A.D. in western Europe. During this time, the most powerful people were kings and great lords, called nobles, who ruled over large areas of land.

Nobles granted pieces of their land, called manors, to lesser nobles. The lesser nobles promised to advise their lords and to fight against their enemies. Peasants farmed the land, while people in towns worked at various **trades** and professions, including carpentry, shoemaking, law, and banking.

During the Middle Ages, family members worked together in the fields, in shops, and in the home. They also took care of each other, especially of the young, the sick, and the elderly.

▶ *In return for being cared for, children were expected to love and obey their parents and act in a way that made their parents proud.*

Arabs introduce chess to Europe
800s

Towns start building free elementary schools; toy tops appear in England
1000

Young people and poor people travel to the Holy Land on "the Children's Crusade"
1212

Toymaking is a full-time trade in Germany
1400s

900s
Playing cards invented in China

1200s
First village schools set up to teach peasant children; first universities established

1365
Playing ball games discouraged in England; young men practice war games instead

1429
Seventeen-year-old Joan of Arc leads French troops against English invaders

▲ *Children around the world played different games in the Middle Ages. For example, children in England played soccer, in West Africa they wrestled, and in the **Middle East** they played polo.*

From Child to Adult

Very young children spent their days playing with toys, making up games, and having fun. Around the age of seven, children started to have lessons to learn and chores to do. By the age of twelve or fourteen, children were considered young adults and were expected to work.

▶ *Where children lived, what education they received, and what toys they played with depended on their parents' place in society. Kings and great lords were considered the most important people in **medieval** times, while peasants, who made up 90 percent of the population, were considered the least important.*

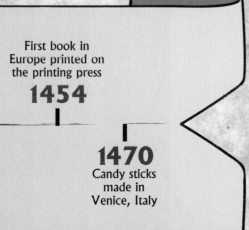

First book in Europe printed on the printing press

1454

1470
Candy sticks made in Venice, Italy

Babies

In the Middle Ages, babies and very young children were cared for by their mothers, by servants, and by nurses. Babies were born at home surrounded by female family members, friends, and sometimes a midwife, who was a local woman trained to deliver babies.

Newborn babies were swaddled, which means they were wrapped tightly in cloth to keep them warm. Babies also wore diapers made of cloth rags, undershirts, bonnets, bibs, and booties. Mothers bathed their babies in small buckets or pots, with water and homemade soap. After the babies were bathed, the bath water was used to wash the babies' dirty diapers and clothes.

A Baby's Food

Most medieval mothers breastfed their babies for two or three years. Noblewomen and the wives of wealthy **merchants** often hired wet nurses, who fed the babies their own breast milk.

Once they were old enough, babies ate soft food such as pap, a porridge made of bread mixed with milk or water. They also ate mashed fruit, vegetables, and hard-boiled eggs, or adult food that their mothers or nurses chewed into a mush.

◄ *Swaddling prevented babies from falling out of cradles, and some people believed it helped make babies' arms and legs grow straight.*

Baby Furniture

At night, babies slept in rocking cradles beside their mothers' beds. During the day, they slept in cradles beside cooking fires. Baby furniture also included crickets, which were small stools mothers sat on while rocking cradles. Children sat on the crickets when they were older.

▶ *Standing stools, or frames, helped toddlers learn to walk.*

Dangers in Homes

Dangers were always present in medieval homes. Children burned themselves on cooking fires, choked on the fires' smoke, or fell off stools, chairs, and tables. Outside, they drowned in streams, rivers, and wells, were trampled by animals, or were run over by plows and carts.

The greatest dangers to children in the Middle Ages were deadly, contagious diseases, such as the Plague, and illnesses, such as pneumonia and the flu. Most sicknesses could not be cured by medieval medicine, and many young children died. Babies also died in childbirth, as did their mothers. Between one quarter and one third of medieval children did not reach the age of one.

▲ *A medieval doctor treats a family for the Plague. Symptoms of the Plague included red spots on the skin, painful black bulges under the arms, vomiting, headaches, fever, and coughing up blood.*

Toys and Games

Children in the Middle Ages played with toys. Dice, marbles, swords, balls, and dolls were made at home from rags, candle wax, animal bones, sticks, and stones. Rattles, puppets, and spinning tops were made of metal and wood by craftspeople in towns.

▶ *Hobby horses and rocking horses were very popular among noble children. They were colorfully painted and decorated to look like real horse heads.*

▼ *Aboriginal peoples who lived in the cold, northern parts of North America made darts and spears that they slid across snow and ice in a game called "snow snake."*

◀ *Girls played with the same toys as boys, but they also liked puppets, which are now called dolls. The puppets were made of clay, wax, wool, or wood, and they were painted and dressed in various costumes. Peasant girls had puppets dressed in work clothes, while noble girls had puppets in fancy headdresses and long robes.*

▶ *Children from wealthy families played with board games, such as checkers.*

Games of All Kinds

Board games, such as chess, were popular in the Middle Ages. Chess's rules and game pieces, such as the king, queen, **bishops**, and **knights**, taught children about different people's roles in society. Children learned these games from their parents, who often played them with their friends.

Medieval children and adults also played games similar to bowling, badminton, tennis, soccer, baseball, and golf. Balls were usually made of leather stuffed with horsehair or of dried pigs' **bladders** filled with dried peas.

Summer was the time for swimming in rivers and lakes. Life preservers made of tree bark helped young children stay afloat. In the winter, children played ice sports similar to **curling** and hockey. Skates were made from sharpened cattle or horse bones tied to children's shoes.

War Games

Horseback riding, archery, wrestling, and a game called sword and **buckler**, which involved pretend sword fights, prepared noble boys for knightly combat, as did hunting in the manor's forests. While their parents hunted deer and wild boar with hunting dogs, noble children caught birds and other small animals with hawks and falcons. Less wealthy children hunted small animals with traps and homemade bows and arrows.

◀ *Boys playing with bows and arrows learned the skills they would need to go to war or to hunt.*

9

Having Fun

Many of the games children play today were also played in the Middle Ages. Guessing games, such as heads or tails, running games, such as hide-and-seek, and circle games, such as "Ring Around the Rosies," which is based on a rhyme about the Plague, were popular. Children also enjoyed folk dancing and playing musical instruments, such as tambourines, bells, drums, flutes, harps, and bagpipes.

1 **2** **3** **4** Children often walked on stilts, gave each other piggyback rides, wrestled, and climbed trees.

5 **6** **7** **8** Marbles and dice, balls, hoops and sticks, and make-believe swords were popular toys.

9 **10** **11** Girls and boys played games together, such as tag, leapfrog, and hopscotch.

Peasant Children

Peasant children spent their days helping their parents grow food, raise livestock, and do chores. They lived in small cottages that were often dark, because there were few windows, and smoky, because food was cooked over open fires in the main room.

Peasant homes did not have a lot of furniture, usually just a few stools and a trestle table, which was a board set up on two supports, on which the family ate meals. The trestle table was taken down at night to make room for the straw mats on which the family slept. Some peasant homes had a loft for sleeping, which the family reached by climbing up a ladder. Farm animals often lived inside peasants' homes, in pens separated from the main room by a small wall.

▶ *Some peasants kept livestock behind their homes, such as sheep, which were used for meat and their wool.*

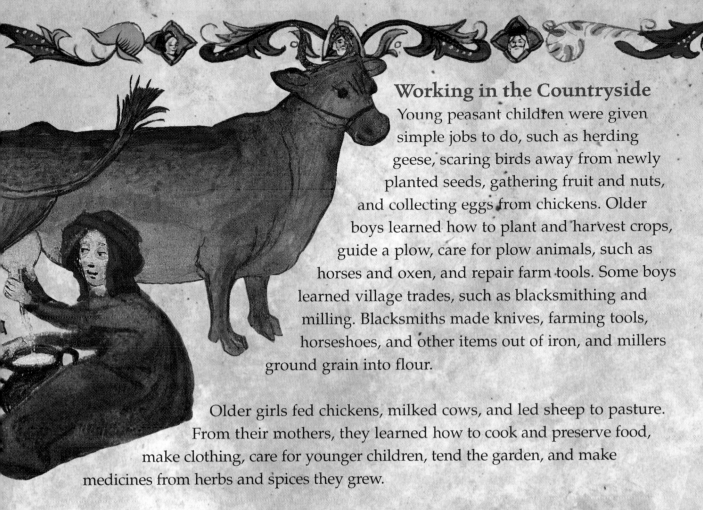

Working in the Countryside

Young peasant children were given simple jobs to do, such as herding geese, scaring birds away from newly planted seeds, gathering fruit and nuts, and collecting eggs from chickens. Older boys learned how to plant and harvest crops, guide a plow, care for plow animals, such as horses and oxen, and repair farm tools. Some boys learned village trades, such as blacksmithing and milling. Blacksmiths made knives, farming tools, horseshoes, and other items out of iron, and millers ground grain into flour.

Older girls fed chickens, milked cows, and led sheep to pasture. From their mothers, they learned how to cook and preserve food, make clothing, care for younger children, tend the garden, and make medicines from herbs and spices they grew.

▲ *Peasant children had chores to do every day. Girls milked cows for milk that was used to make butter and cheese.*

In the Manor House

Some peasant children moved to towns and cities to learn a trade. Others worked as servants in the manor house, where the noble who ruled the manor lived. Boys worked in the kitchen as turnspits, turning meat on skewers over the fire, and as scullions, washing dishes. Stable boys cleaned out the stables and kennel boys took care of the hunting dogs. Girls usually worked as maids, cleaning, doing the laundry, and mending clothes.

▶ *During harvest time, which was very busy for peasant families, children helped pick fresh fruits from the orchards.*

Children in Towns

During the Middle Ages, towns grew to be busy places. Wealthy merchants, lawyers, and bankers lived there, as well as craftspeople and tradespeople who made food, clothing, and household items.

Children from wealthy town families lived in large houses with their parents, brothers and sisters, and servants. Children from less wealthy families lived in smaller houses or apartments above their parents' workshops. Their households included their parents, siblings, and often their fathers' **apprentices**.

▲ *Families in towns ate in the main room of their home. Meals included roasted meats served with bread, cheese, and wine.*

Preparing for Work

Some children of bankers, merchants, and other professional townspeople attended school from the age of seven to twelve. Then, they worked for five to ten years with their fathers as apprentices.

Girls from wealthy families were taught by their mothers how to run a household, which included managing the household's money and servants. They also learned how to cook, sew, weave, embroider, and take care of children.

◀ *Young children learned trades, such as carpentry, by working in their fathers' shops collecting wood scraps.*

Learning a Trade

The children of shoemakers, tailors, **armorers,** and other craftspeople did not usually attend school. Instead, they apprenticed for their fathers, learning the family trade. Some parents paid masters, who were expert craftspeople or tradespeople, to hire their children as apprentices. The children usually left home between the ages of twelve and fourteen to live and work in the masters' homes.

An Apprentice's Work

Much of an apprentice's time was spent watching the master at work and doing small jobs, such as cleaning the shop and the tools. Eventually, the apprentice began working as the master's assistant. A painter's assistant, for example, mixed paint at first, but was not allowed to paint anything. Apprentices were given more responsibilities as they learned their trades.

After about seven years of work, apprentices became journeymen. Journeymen often traveled and worked for different masters to gain experience. When they were ready, they showed their finest piece of work to an organization of craftworkers or tradespeople called a guild. If the guild members decided that the work was good enough, the journeyman was granted the title of "master." The master could then open his own shop and hire his own apprentices.

◀ *An apprentice in the workshop of a cooper, or barrel maker, helped the master by fetching water and tools and by cleaning the workshop.*

Becoming a Knight

Young noble children lived in castles or manor houses with their parents, their brothers and sisters, and their fathers' advisors, knights, and servants. Castles were built for defense, not for comfort, and were often cold, drafty places.

A castle's main room was the Great Hall. Children enjoyed feasts in the Great Hall and, in the early Middle Ages, slept there with their families, separated from other castle residents by a curtain. In the later Middle Ages, children either slept in their parents' bedrooms or in their own rooms. Many had fancy beds, with headboards and footboards, and curtains surrounding them to keep out drafts.

Pages

Noble boys were usually sent to other noble households to learn how to be knights. They began their training as pages around the age of seven. They served food in the Great Hall and were trained by the castle's soldiers to take care of weapons, use wooden and blunted weapons, and ride and care for horses.

▼ *Noble boys training to be knights learned how to fight with swords, spears, and shields.*

From Squires to Knights

Pages became squires around the age of fourteen. They learned how to use real weapons, such as daggers, **maces**, shields, **lances**, and swords. Squires also learned archery and **fencing**.

Between the ages of eighteen and twenty-one, a squire became a knight. During a ceremony called a dubbing, the knight knelt before the lord, who tapped his shoulder with a flat sword. Then, the knight received his own sword as a symbol of knighthood.

◄ *A squire's main job was to take care of a knight's weapons and horses. He also dressed the knight for battle or for a tournament, which was a contest of skill between knights.*

Becoming a Samurai

In Japan in the Middle Ages, young noblemen trained to become warriors called samurai. They learned how to ride horseback, use weapons such as bows, arrows, and long swords called tachi, and perform **martial arts**. They also learned how to survive in the wild and how to hunt. Samurai had to follow a strict code of behavior, known as bushido, which included bravery, honor, loyalty, honesty, and self-discipline.

▶ *Like medieval knights, samurai wore suits of chain mail and plate armor.*

Becoming a Lady

Most noble girls were taught by their mothers how to dress and behave like proper noblewomen. This included learning how to sew, weave, and embroider; how to read, write, and pray; and how to ride horses and hunt.

Noble girls were also taught how to run a noble's household and defend the castle when the noble was away. They also learned simple medical care, such as bandaging wounds, soothing burns, setting broken limbs, cleaning and sewing up cuts, and making medicine from herbs grown in the castle or manor house's garden.

▶ *Nobles' homes often had chapels where the families prayed. Prayers were said in Latin, the language of ancient Romans and of educated people in Middle Ages.*

▼ *Noblewomen on horseback joined in the hunt, chasing animals such as deer and wild boars.*

Ladies-in-Waiting

Some girls were sent to another noble's home to be trained by the lady of the house. In return, the noble girl acted as a lady-in-waiting. She helped the noble lady bathe and dress, read stories to her, traveled with her, attended **Mass** with her, and cared for her when she was sick or having a baby.

Getting Married

Noble girls as young as age twelve became engaged to boys from other noble families. The marriages were arranged between a girl's parents and a boy's parents to join two important families. The boy and girl often did not know one another before they were engaged.

When a noble girl married, she, like all other girls, received gifts from her parents. The gifts, which were called a dowry, consisted of clothing, furniture, linen, jewelry, and money. The girl used these items to start her own home.

▼ *Rings were exchanged at the wedding ceremony. They were worn on the third finger of the left hand, now called "the ring finger," since medieval people believed a vein ran from that finger to the heart.*

Clothing

Young children in the Middle Ages wore clothing similar to that of their parents. Boys wore loose garments, called tunics, that usually came down to their knees, while girls wore tunics that reached their ankles. Socks or stockings covered their legs, and all but the poorest children wore leather shoes.

By the later Middle Ages, styles changed, especially for wealthy boys in their early teens. They wore hip-length jackets, called doublets, and hose, which covered their legs from their waists to their toes.

▼ *Peasant children wore tunics, cloaks, and woolen socks, which they rolled down in the summer heat.*

Material for Clothing

Clothing in the Middle Ages was usually made of wool, which children's mothers spun by hand. Peasant children's clothes were dyed dull brown, green, and yellow, with dyes made from plants grown locally. Peasant children often had only one set of clothes which their mothers and older sisters mended and cleaned at night.

Wealthier children's clothing was made of finer wool, silk, and velvet. It was often dyed bright red, green, and blue, with dyes made from plants that came from the Middle East, China, and India. The clothing was very expensive, and was often passed down from one generation to the next.

◀ *The sons of nobles and wealthy townspeople wore linen undergarments and long woolen tunics with leather or jeweled belts.*

▶ *Spinning, or turning wool into thread, was a trade that all girls learned. Peasant girls who did not marry often earned a living by spinning. That is the origin of the word "spinster," once used to describe a woman who lived on her own and never married.*

Keeping Clean

People in the Middle Ages kept as clean as they could with little running water and mostly homemade soaps.

Children washed their hands before and after each meal, since they usually ate with their fingers. They usually bathed in wooden barrels filled with water drawn from nearby wells or rivers. The water was sometimes heated over a fire. Towns had bathhouses where people paid to bathe in barrels large enough for four to six people.

Most children in the Middle Ages washed with soap that their mothers made from animal fat and ashes. Wealthier children used gentler soaps and shampoos made of olive oil and pleasant smelling herbs, which merchants brought from far away.

Brushing Teeth and Hair

Peasant children cleaned their teeth with a cloth and used twigs or thread to remove food stuck between their teeth. Wealthier children brushed their teeth with a homemade toothpaste made of flour, a metal called alum, some honey, and a bit of mint. They used twigs or their fingers as toothbrushes. They brushed their hair with combs made of wood, bone, or expensive ivory. Lice, a common problem in the Middle Ages, were removed with a specially made shampoo.

▲ *In the summer, children bathed in rivers, streams, and ponds or in barrels placed outdoors.*

Education

Many boys from wealthy families in towns went to school, even if it was only for a year. Noble children had tutors in the castle or manor home.

Children learned the basics of reading and writing, simple arithmetic, and enough Latin to say their prayers. Most teachers were male, but there were some female teachers. Male teachers were called masters, and female teachers were called mistresses.

Good students continued their education for many years, and the brightest male students attended university. The first universities were established in the Middle Ages.

▲ *Some girls were taught to read by private female tutors, called mistresses.*

▼ *Students sat around the master's chair on benches, on stools, or on the floor, which was covered by rugs, straw, or dirt.*

Medieval Schools

There were different types of schools in the Middle Ages. In towns, teachers ran private schools from their homes, charging a fee to educate the children of wealthy townspeople.

Some of the best schools in the Middle Ages were church schools. Church schools had well-educated teachers who could teach more difficult subjects and prepare students for university. The schools were held in cathedrals, which were the main churches in an area, in **monasteries**, or in **convents**. The students were usually the children of wealthy townspeople and nobles whose families made donations to the schools, but some less wealthy students were also taught there.

By 1000, a few town governments had set up free schools. Some local priests also ran schools for peasant children in villages. Lessons were not given during the harvest season, when the children were busy helping in the fields.

▼ Students who boarded, or lived, at monastery schools had to follow rules about what to wear, when to pray, and how to behave.

Advertisement by a Schoolmaster

Many schoolmasters advertised for students by hanging signs on the front doors of their homes. The signs read like this one: "I am a good schoolmaster in the city, who will teach you how to read and write well, and to count numbers. I will teach you well without trickery. I teach the poor for God, and the rich for money. Come all, quickly!"

School Supplies

Students learned to write by scratching words on wood tablets covered with leather, wax, bark, or **parchment**. They wrote with a stylus, which was a thin, pointed stick, or a goose quill dipped in ink. Children learned to count using their fingers, marbles, or an abacus, an instrument with wires along which beads were slid.

Not many students owned books because they were very expensive. Instead, they used the schools' library books, which were chained to the bookshelves so they would not be stolen. Teachers often complained that students ruined books by eating and drinking near them and by getting the pages wet with their runny noses.

◀ *Some classrooms used blackboards to teach students how to read and write.*

Universities

Only male students were allowed to attend university. They studied grammar, logic, rhetoric, which is the art of speech making, then arithmetic, geometry, **astronomy**, and music. Some students went on to study law, medicine, or religion.

The first universities were classrooms in masters' homes. Students lived in rented rooms nearby. Eventually, wealthy people built classrooms, **dormitories**, and libraries, and **scholars** joined together to form universities similar to those of today. The first universities in western Europe, the University of Paris, in France, and the University of Bologna, in Italy, were established in the early 1200s.

Education Around the World

Europe was not the only place with schools of higher education. **Muslim** boys in the West African city of Timbuktu studied law, history, and their religion, Islam. Aztec boys from noble families went to school in the capital of Tenochtitlan, now Mexico City, to learn reading, writing, arithmetic, astronomy, and religion.

The Church

Some children in the Middle Ages devoted their lives to the Roman Catholic Church. **Boys became priests and monks, and girls became nuns.**

Priests

Young men could become priests when they were 24 years old and had passed exams testing their knowledge of prayers and Mass. Priests led religious services at local churches, performed marriages and burials, and gave advice to members of the community.

Monks

Boys sometimes trained to be monks. Monks devoted their lives to prayer and study. They lived apart from society in monasteries, where they had to follow certain rules, including giving up all their possessions and spending their days in silence.

▲ Boys helped out in the church by reading the Bible, singing prayers, lighting candles, and ringing bells during Mass.

▼ Monks copied books onto parchment and drew beautiful designs, called illuminations, on the pages with quill pens and inks of different colors. After cities developed, beautiful illuminations were also produced by artisans for noble and wealthy families.

Working in the Monastery

In addition to praying and studying, monks copied important books, such as the Bible, worked in the monastery's gardens where they grew herbs to make medicines, or took care of visitors to the monastery, including the sick and elderly. Many monasteries owned large manors, which monks managed.

Nuns

Nuns are religious women who live in convents apart from society. In the Middle Ages, some girls entered convents because they wanted to devote their lives to God, get a good education, or avoid marriage, since nuns are not allowed to marry. Other girls were placed in convents because their parents could not find them husbands or afford dowries.

In convents, girls read, sang, prayed, and performed church services. They copied and illuminated books, and spun, wove, and sewed beautiful clothes for church services. Some girls became highly educated nuns. They offered spiritual advice to convent visitors, worked as teachers at convent schools, and worked as nurses in convent **infirmaries**. Nuns also managed the lands that the convents owned.

The Children's Crusade

From about 1096 to 1291, Christians traveled to the **Holy Land** to fight a series of wars called the crusades. They were trying to regain control of holy sites from Muslims who ruled the area. Some young people and poor families were so devoted to the Church that they went on a "Children's Crusade" in 1212. The crusade was a disaster. Most families never even made it to the Holy Land, but got stranded in Italy. Greedy merchants lured some of the stranded children onto ships and sold them into slavery in North Africa. The **Pope**, fearing for the young people's safety, sent many of them back home.

Holidays

The word "holiday" comes from "holy day," a special day in the Christian Church. Christmas and Easter were among the holiest days in medieval times.

Christmas

Christmas remembers the day when Jesus Christ, who Christians believe is God's son on earth, was born. People in the Middle Ages decorated their homes for Christmas with ivy, holly, mistletoe, and other greenery. Nobles invited peasants for a large meal of meat, soup, good bread, and ale or wine. Meanwhile, nobles held separate feasts for other nobles, in which elaborate dishes, such as roasted peacock and boar, were served.

▲ *During the winter, many people, especially peasants, had less work to do. They enjoyed their free time by having snowball fights and building snowmen with their children.*

Medieval Gingerbread

People in the Middle Ages ate gingerbread as Christmas treats. To make tasty medieval gingerbread, boil four cups (one liter) of honey in a pot. Skim the scum off the top. On low heat, stir in one pound (0.45 kilograms) of unseasoned bread crumbs and one tablespoon (fifteen milliliters) each of ginger, cinnamon, and ground white pepper. Add a few drops of red food coloring if you like. Stir while cooking. When the batter thickens, remove it from the heat and let it cool slightly. Then, pour the batter on a flat surface and press it firmly into a square about one inch (2.5 centimeters) thick. Let cool, then cut into small squares to serve.

Easter

At Easter, people in the Middle Ages remembered the death and resurrection, or return to life, of Jesus. On the Friday and Saturday before Easter, children ran through the streets with rattles called clappers, calling people to prayer. On Easter Sunday, church bells rang out in celebration.

Children played games on Easter. They painted and exchanged brightly decorated Easter eggs with one another, and rolled the eggs down hills to see whose could get to the bottom the fastest without cracking. Children also chased hens, trying to be the first to catch one. **Mystery plays** were also popular entertainment for children at Easter.

Saints' Days and Halloween

In medieval times, many villages and towns had patron **saints** who were believed to protect the people who lived there. Special holidays, called saints' days, celebrated the lives of the saints. Villagers and townspeople went to church and watched plays and puppet shows that depicted stories from the saints' lives.

All Saints' Day, November 1, honored all Christian saints. The night before All Saints' Day was called All Hallow's Eve, or Halloween. It was celebrated with apple-bobbing contests, candlelight parades, and masked children asking for cakes.

▶ *On saints' days, people paraded through churches and streets with statues or relics of the saints. Children also dressed up as priests and bishops and went from house to house asking for money or food.*

Markets, Fairs, and Festivals

Market days, fairs, and festivals were times of celebration in the Middle Ages. On market days, townspeople and nearby villagers gathered to buy and sell fruits, vegetables, livestock, clothing, and household goods.

Markets were full of treats for children. Bakers made sweet pies, pastries, and fancy biscuits, and local craftspeople sold toy tops, whistles, and clay dolls.

Fairs

Fairs were very large markets that were held once a year, usually around a saint's day. At fairs, children passed by booths that sold goods from far away. There were mirrors from France, furs from Russia, puppets and other toys from Germany, and oranges, pomegranates, and sugar from the Middle East. Children were also entertained by jugglers tossing balls and fire sticks, acrobats leaping and somersaulting, trained bears and monkeys tumbling and dancing, and musicians performing on bagpipes, flutes, drums, fiddles, and small harps.

Children enjoyed a break from chores on festival days, spending their time playing games such as leapfrog.

Harvest Time

Harvest time was celebrated with feasts, dancing, and games. On the Feast of the Plowman, celebrated on November 11, lords invited peasants to their castles and manor homes for elaborate meals made from wheat the peasants had harvested. Breads, cakes, and puddings were served. During the holiday, boys from different schools competed in sailing, wrestling, and sports such as field hockey and soccer. Younger children received gifts of apples and nuts as they paraded through the streets singing.

▶ *Peasants enjoyed the abundance of food during the harvest season, but they also preserved extra food for the long winter ahead.*

May Day

On May Day, May 1, villagers celebrated the arrival of spring. They decorated a tall pole, called the Maypole, with colorful ribbons and flowers. Then, they chose a May Queen and May King, who danced around the pole with other children to the music of flutes and fiddles.

▼ *During festive times of the year, medieval people enjoyed carol dancing, where they held hands and danced in a circle around a singer.*

Church Ales

Church ales were celebrations at the village church where members sold ale they brewed themselves. They used the money they raised to repair the church and help the poor. Feasts accompanied the celebrations.

Glossary

apprentice A person learning a trade from someone more experienced

armorer A person who makes weapons and clothing that protects soldiers during battle

artisan A skilled craftsperson

astronomy The study of the stars and planets

bishop A chess piece named after a high-ranking leader of the Catholic Church

bladder A sac within an animal that holds urine

buckler A small, round hand-held shield

convent A home for nuns, or women devoted to the Catholic Church

curling A game in which players slide heavy stones toward the center of a circle at the other end of an ice rink

dormitory A room with sleeping quarters for several people

fencing The sport of fighting with long, thin swords

Holy Land An area in present-day Israel, Jordan, and Syria that has special religious meaning for Christians, Muslims, and Jews

infirmary A place where sick or injured people are cared for

knight A chess piece named after a warrior who fought on horseback, mainly with swords

lance A long, wooden pole with a sharp iron or steel head

livestock Farm animals

mace A heavy club with a spiked metal head, used to crush armor

martial art A sport that uses warlike techniques for self-defense and exercise

Mass The main ceremony of the Roman Catholic Church

medieval Relating to the Middle Ages

merchant A person who buys and sells goods

Middle East A region made up of southwestern Asia and northern Africa

monastery A community where religious men called monks live and work

Muslim A person who believes in Islam, which is a religion based on the teachings of Allah and his prophets

mystery play A medieval play based on a story from the Bible

parchment The skin of a sheep or goat on which people write or paint

Pope The leader of the Roman Catholic Church

relic Something that belonged to a holy person, such as clothing or a body part

Roman Catholic Church The Christian Church led by the pope in Rome

saint A person through whom God performs miracles, according to the Christian Church

scholar A very knowledgeable person

trade A type of business, usually one that involves working with the hands

Index

2 3 4 5 6 7 8 9 0   Printed in the U.S.A.   0 9 8 7 6 5